Copyright © 2025 Clavis Publishing Inc., New York

Originally published as *Wetenschap op wielen* in Belgium and the Netherlands by Clavis Uitgeverij, 2025
English translation from the Dutch by Clavis Publishing Inc., New York

Visit us on the Web at www.clavis-publishing.com.

No part of this publication may be reproduced or stored in a retrieval system,
or transmitted in any form or by any means, electronic, mechanical, photocopying,
recording, or otherwise, without the prior written permission of the publisher,
except in the case of brief quotations embodied in critical articles and reviews.
For information regarding permissions, write to Clavis Publishing,
info-US@clavisbooks.com. Text and data mining are not allowed.

Science Takes a Trip written by Maria Rentetzi and illustrated by Pieter De Decker

ISBN 979-8-89063-245-6

This book was printed in May 2025 at Guangzhou Zhongtian Colour Printing Co., Ltd.
No. 6, Xihuan Road, Shilou Twon, Panyu District, Guangzhou 511447, China.

First Edition
10 9 8 7 6 5 4 3 2 1

Clavis Publishing supports the First Amendment and celebrates the right to read.

Science Takes a Trip

Written by Maria Rentetzi
Illustrated by Pieter De Decker

NEW YORK

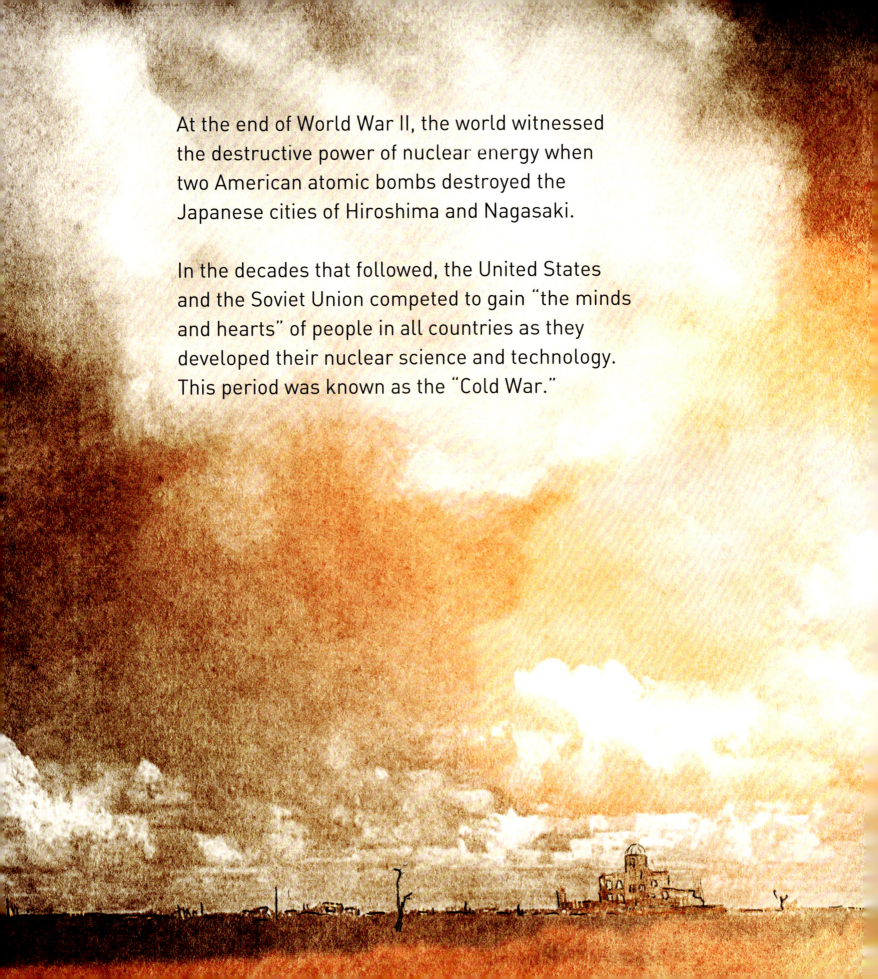

At the end of World War II, the world witnessed the destructive power of nuclear energy when two American atomic bombs destroyed the Japanese cities of Hiroshima and Nagasaki.

In the decades that followed, the United States and the Soviet Union competed to gain "the minds and hearts" of people in all countries as they developed their nuclear science and technology. This period was known as the "Cold War."

The United States wanted to show the world that atomic energy could, first and foremost, be used for good. Its use could bring progress and prosperity to humanity.

In 1958, President Eisenhower donated two new blue buses that held complete working laboratories to the International Atomic Energy Agency (IAEA). These "laboratories on wheels" would help train scientists around the world. In these labs, scientists could work with radioisotopes and apply atomic energy in medicine, agriculture, and industry.

While the scientists learned about the uses of nuclear energy, they also became reliant on American technologies. This was a way for the US to get ahead in the Cold War.

The first lab, over thirty feet long and weighing thirteen tons, went to Europe by freighter. Its mission began at the Atoms for Peace exhibition in Geneva, Switzerland. The ambassadors and scientists in attendance found this mobile laboratory fascinating.

Then the lab went to the IAEA headquarters in Vienna, Austria. The agency's director, Sterling Cole, was quite impressed. He held an inauguration ceremony for the traveling science station. Distinguished ladies and gentlemen, scientists, ambassadors, and photographers waited patiently to admire the tools and equipment inside.

In Austria, the team held the first training sessions in the lab, which consisted of a chemical laboratory and a radiation measurement chamber. The lab had enough space to train six scientists at the same time.

The mobile unit headed to Athens in 1959. On the way to Greece, its wheels got stuck in the mud on a rural road. A day later, trying to cross a narrow wooden bridge, the lab got stuck again, making for an exhausting trip. Moving scientific knowledge was not an easy task.

In Athens, the team scrubbed the battered blue bus until it shone in the sun. Scientists from a hospital happily climbed aboard to research ways of diagnosing diseases.

Next, the lab toured five cities in Yugoslavia, offering training to engineers and technicians. The last stop in Europe was the West German city of Essen.

In 1960, the lab went to Asia by ship. Upon reaching Seoul, South Korea, one of its wheels needed to be replaced. The ocean journey had taken a toll on the sturdy vehicle.

The traveling team typically visited big cities to train people at universities. But there were also tiny villages in need of new technologies. If there were no roads, the lab had to go by train or take another ship. These rural visits allowed scientists in remote areas to gain access to modern innovations.

The following year, Taiwan, the Philippines, and Indonesia all hosted the US team and its laboratory. In each country, the traveling scientists tailored the training sessions to people's needs. Everywhere it went, the mobile lab opened its door to fellow scientists, with or without lab coats, with or without shoes.

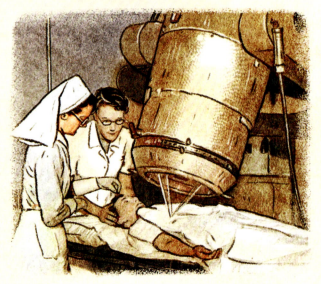

In 1962, the laboratory went to Vietnam for six months; the next year, it stopped in Singapore for a while. The training sessions taught local scientists to use atomic energy safely for many things. It could help fight cancer, keep potatoes fresh longer, increase rice harvests, and even protect fruit trees from pests.

The last trip this mobile lab made was to Africa. In Ghana, young scientists had the chance to do experiments with radioisotopes and learn about radiation risks.

After each stop, the bus became a bit more colorful. That's because the team painted the flags of each country they visited on its door.

But wait—weren't there two mobile laboratories? Indeed, there were!

The second blue bus stayed in the Americas. In 1960, it began its tour of Latin America in Mexico. It then went to Argentina, Uruguay, Brazil, and Bolivia to train students in the applications of radioisotopes in medicine. Finally, in Costa Rica, it helped the locals eradicate a fruit fly infestation.

The long journey of the two mobile laboratories was a unique project of the IAEA. Moving scientific knowledge through continents became an adventure due to border controls, unexpected weather conditions, narrow streets, running out of gas, and much, much more. But sharing knowledge around the world made it all worthwhile.

Two Blue Mobile Laboratories

In the late 1950s, the United States, under President Dwight D. Eisenhower, donated two mobile laboratories to the International Atomic Energy Agency (IAEA). The IAEA was newly established in 1957 at the suggestion of the United States and as part of Atoms for Peace, a program to control nuclear energy and its industrial exploitation on a global scale.

The first director of the IAEA, Sterling Cole, used the two laboratories to train scientists around the world in the application of radioisotopes and radiation protection methods. Sending the two mobile laboratories to four continents was one of the largest technical assistance projects of the IAEA and the first major project in its history.

The buses housing the laboratories were painted blue to match the radiation symbol at the time, also known as the "trefoil" for its three-part design. Originally, this design was a magenta symbol on a blue background. It was soon changed to black and yellow for greater visibility, but the buses remained blue.

Photographs from that time show the economic inequality on the planet, but they also paint a picture of global hope for peace and prosperity.